Tax Season Profitability Guide
8 Big Ideas For A More Profitable Tax Season

Jassen Bowman, EA

TaxMarketingHQ.com

Copyright © 2013 Jassen Bowman
All rights reserved.

IMPORTANT NOTICE

This book is designed to provide accurate and authoritative information in regards to the subject matter covered, but it is sold with the understanding that the publisher is not engaged in rendering legal or accounting services, and no information contained herein should be construed as legal advice.

If legal advice or other expert assistance is required, the services of a competent professional person should be sought. The publisher does not guarantee or warrant that readers who use the information provided in this publication will achieve results similar to those discussed.

While every effort has been taken to ensure that the information contained herein is accurate as of the time of publication, tax laws and regulations are constantly changing.

The applicability of the marketing strategies discussed in this book may vary depending upon your skill set, the geographical location of your practice, economic factors, your target market, and other factors that are beyond the control of the author and publisher. Any income examples used in this publication are for illustrative purposes only, and are not a guarantee of income, nor are they necessarily representative of specific tax professionals.

Like all things in life, your results and success in business are directly connected to your own motivation and level of action. The strategies described in this book do work, but they only work if you *take action* to make them work. Nobody else can make you successful, you must take the actions necessary to get there; this book is just a roadmap.

This page intentionally left blank. But putting that message makes it no longer blank, so why is it convention to put an "intentionally left blank" message on a page that is no longer blank?

FREE BONUS

This book is really just the beginning of your journey. In order to support you in your efforts at growing your tax practice, we created a **membership website** that has additional training and resources to help you build your tax resolution practice.

The great news is that access to this site is 100% free. To get access, go to:

www.TaxMarketingHQ.com/bonus

Here is what you'll receive:

- A comprehensive 6-hour video series that introduces you to the essentials of starting and growing a tax resolution practice, including the fundamentals of marketing, client intake, practice management, sales, and tax resolution case work.
- Detailed training on how to find your first tax resolution client.
- How to quote tax resolution fees.
- The world famous *One-Hour Per Day Marketing Plan*.
- Access to complimentary CE/CPE webinars on IRS Collections topics.
- Additional links, resources, and bonuses from the book.
- A few surprises along the way.

You can access everything at:

https://TaxMarketingHQ.com/bonus

Please note that this offer is subject to change or substitution at any time.

TABLE OF CONTENTS

Free Bonus v

Preface: The Hidden Profits Inside Your Existing Tax Practice 1

Big idea #1: There Are Only Three Ways to Boost Firm Profits 3

Big Idea #2: It's Easier & Cheaper to Keep Old Clients Than to Attract New Ones 11

Big Idea #3: Direct Mail Is Far From Dead 25

Big Idea #4: Leverage Professional Relationships 41

Big Idea #5: Ask For Referrals 49

Big Idea#6: Choose Thy Clients Wisely 51

Big Idea #7: Raise Your Fees 55

Big Idea #8: Increase Efficiency Via Systems 63

Profitability Is A Choice 69

About the Author 71

Free Bonus 73

PREFACE: THE HIDDEN PROFITS INSIDE YOUR EXISTING TAX PRACTICE

Your license to practice is a license to print money.

As a CPA, EA, or tax attorney in private practice, the government has, for all intents and purposes, handed you the ability to legally print money.

Think about it for a minute. No matter which party controls either chamber of Congress or the controls the Oval Office… Regardless of who sits in command of Treasury or the IRS… No matter what the economy is doing… Regardless of what revenue procedures and other guidance emerge for the Tax Cuts & Jobs Act…

…the fact is that U.S. tax laws are *exhaustive and exhausting*. That means **money in your pocket**.

While the technology to fully automate the preparation of the vast majority of returns is rapidly maturing, automated bookkeeping is on the horizon, and AI-driven continuous audit is already here, there is still **massive profit potential** within the tax and accounting landscape.

The future of your firm will ultimately have less focus on reporting and compliance, and more focus on structuring, consulting, and advising, but for the next several years, the right clients will still rely on you heavily to guide them through the maze of the Internal Revenue Code and the bureaucratic insanity of government agencies. There will continue to be profits to extract from this activity for at least the next few years. The big ideas presented in this book are intended to help you maximize your profits from offerings your services in that arena.

In the future, as you transition into other services that are less focused on compliance and more focused on advisory, you will continue to profit from the big ideas in this book. In fact, they will actually become even more important, because issues such as client selection, value-based pricing, and a systems approach to operations are much more critical to a **highly specialized, niche consulting practice**.

It is my sincere hope that you embrace, internalize, and act upon the principles contained herein. Rather than just being a book that you skim through and throw on the shelf, please refer back to this book frequently. Perhaps work on one big idea per month or quarter, cycling through them on a rotating basis to elevate your practice over time.

To your profitability,

Jassen Bowman, EA

BIG IDEA #1: THERE ARE ONLY THREE WAYS TO BOOST FIRM PROFITS

When it comes to hitting revenue goals, and formulating the action plan for reaching them, it's important to review the three means of increasing revenue. These three factors are the **only** fundamental ways for a business to make more money:

1. Increase your number of clients.
2. Increase your average fee per client transaction.
3. Increase your number of transactions per client.

That's it. Those are the only three ways that exist for a business of any sort to make more money. **Your written plan to meet your revenue goals needs to incorporate all three.**

Let's consider them further in reverse order.

Increasing your number of transactions per client is quite simple. Your clients already consider you to be a trusted tax expert. As such, they will use your services (or your recommendations for services) for other needs that they may have. Tax professionals should consider offering a variety of additional services that their business and personal clients will find useful. These need to be offered within a cohesive strategy that makes sense for the direction of your practice, but here are some general ideas:

- Payroll service

- Business valuation
- Bookkeeping
- Taxpayer representation (my personal favorite)
- Financial planning/wealth management
- Insurance services
- Tax planning

As an example, there are many tax resolution firms focused primarily on 941 problem resolution that do not offer tax preparation or payroll service, and the three simply go together like peanut butter, jelly, and bread.

Is your practice dominated by 1040 work? Doing high dollar value audit and collections representation, which is a nice niche specialty in which to do highly targeted, aggressive lead generation marketing, is perfect alongside wealth management services and selective tax return preparation.

Specialized bookkeeping and 1040 preparation for real estate investors, combined with property tax valuation dispute services, also makes a nice combination.

Action Question #1: What is your CORE service?

Action Question #2: What <u>package</u> of services could you offer that **complements** your core service?

This coming tax season is the perfect opportunity for you to offer additional services, especially packages of services, to your existing clients. For many practitioners, tax season is the only time of the year that they see most of their clients face to face. This face time is an amazing opportunity to uncover the needs of your clients, and help them by increasing the number of times you see them each year.

If nothing else, and I mean at an absolute minimum, use your face time with clients during tax season to discuss with them the benefits of quarterly or annual tax planning. Even lower income tax clients can benefit from tax planning sometimes, and March/April is a perfect time to set a mid-year appointment, since it's only a couple months away at that point. If you properly educate your clients about the benefits of proactive tax planning, there is a package price that would be of interest to almost anybody.

Next, let's discuss your average fee per client. This book contains an entire chapter dedicated to the discussion of fees, but here's the bottom line on the subject that is applicable to an alarming number of practitioners: **If you haven't raised your fees in years, it's time for you to do so.**

If you're not making the kind of money you want, the first thing you should look at is your fee structure. You'll simply never make $500/hr if your hourly rate is only $125/hr or you're only charging $50 for a 1040. Yes, there are still people that charge this little, even for an itemized 1040. If you're semi-retired or otherwise not interested in making more money, that's your prerogative of course, but I presume that such a practitioner wouldn't be reading this book.

Lastly, let's look at simply getting new clients. The vast majority of information on my blog (TaxMarketingHQ.com) has to do with the subject of lead generation, and most of the Big Ideas presented in this book actually have to do with the subject of getting new clients. So in this section, I want to cover a few items about *improving* your lead generation processes.

If your lead generation campaigns aren't getting you results, here are some things to consider:

1. Do you have an organized, consistent lead generation marketing program in place? prospect follow up system in place?

2. Do you have an organized, consistent prospect follow up marketing system in place?

3. Are you contacting people more than once?

4. Are you contacting lists through multiple methods, such as by direct mail and telephone both?

5. Are you making enough contacts to make statistically valid determinations about the effectiveness of a mail piece, phone script, social media site, etc?

This last one is the biggest mistake I see people make. You can't mail one postcard to the 200 homes closes to your tax office, get zero responses, and say direct mail doesn't work. It's too small of a test to make a valid determination.

When it comes to lead generation, tracking, testing, and measuring are the name of the game. **Track everything, but also do enough of the thing to make it a valid test.**

For example, what's a minimum mailing for determining whether a direct mail campaign is effective or not?

There are a number of rules of thumb about this, and an entire field of statistical analysis in mathematics that studies. Classic texts on direct mail suggest a minimum mailing of 2,000 pieces in order to get any sort of measurable result. My friend James Orr uses a rule of thumb based on dollar expenditure: **$500 minimum to effectively test any mail piece.**

Mathematically speaking, it's hard to make solid determinations about any campaign, piece, media, method, or script until you've received a minimum of 200 "replies". This could mean reaching 200 people on the phone, receiving 200 inquiries via the mail, 200 visitors to a web page, etc.

When I test a new postcard, I don't make any determinations regarding how good or bad it is until I've sent at least 1,000 of them, which will cost around $400. Even then, my determination wouldn't be considered statistically valid by mathematical standards.

This isn't meant to be a stats class, so I hope that you get the general idea. Bottom line is that you must mail a single piece to enough people, or send enough stuff to the same list, in order to properly test the piece.

Similarly, when testing a list, you can't just mail, call, email, or fax it once. You must make multiple contacts in order to properly test the list.

The most important marketing piece you'll ever send is the one following the last one you sent. If you don't have plans in place for the second, third, etc. mailing piece to the same list, then there is no point in sending the first mailing piece -- don't waste your time or money. Repetition and consistency are the keys to a successful marketing plan. One-off, one-shot marketing is marketing suicide. Your marketing message is lost to the person rapidly, so if you don't hit them again, the odds of getting a response are remarkably low.

For the past 80 years, study after study conducted within the direct response marketing circles clearly demonstrates that the majority of responses in a marketing campaign come late in the sequence of marketing messages. The most recent such study that I can find, conducted by Sales and Marketing Executives International a few years ago, clearly demonstrated this. A survey of the organization's members revealed that the number of customers derived from direct mail campaigns looked like this:

After the 1st Contact: 2%
After the 2nd Contact: 4%
After the 3rd Contact: 6%
After the 4th Contact: 10%
After the 5th Contact: 81%

In addition, the survey of SMEI's members indicates that

90% of the time, marketing efforts were abandoned within the first three contacts. In other words, the majority of your competition gives up after three tries, but over 90% of the business is generated AFTER the third try. Think very carefully about this.

I discuss this concept extensively when working with tax professionals to establish their tax resolution services. Most national tax resolution firms only make two or three phone calls when doing telemarketing, and the few that do direct mail only send ONE letter. After a tax lien is filed against a taxpayer, there is a one to two week tidal wave of sales people calling and sending letters from dozens and dozens of big tax resolution firms, and then after that almost NOBODY is contacting them.

The same happens in the tax preparation world. Many tax practitioners send out ONE reminder to their existing clients to schedule an appointment for this next tax season (it's remarkable the number of tax professionals that don't even bother doing that much!). Tax professional that send mailers to new businesses, or new residential movers, or via ValPak/Money Mailer, as examples, often only do it ONCE.

For 1040 services in particular, the advent of Every Door Direct Mail from the US Postal Service makes it simple and affordable to make monthly contact with new movers and entire neighborhoods. There's no excuse not to be doing multiple mailings to your target neighborhoods during tax season.

Take a look at your tax season action plan, and consider

how various combinations of new services, fee increases, and lead generation tweaks will help lead you to your tax season revenue goals.

These sorts of activities should actually take up a substantial amount of your time as a practice owner if you are trying to rapidly grow a practice.

BIG IDEA #2: IT'S EASIER & CHEAPER TO KEEP OLD CLIENTS THAN TO ATTRACT NEW ONES

While the exact number varies by marketing media, the Direct Marketing Association tells us that on average it costs six times more money to acquire a new prospect than to work with one that we already have. When you have a "house list" of people that you already know are interested in your services, no matter how much or how little that level of interest, you are in a far better position to market to that list and achieve a good conversion rate of prospect to client.

The other benefit of working with such a list, rather than a cold list, is that these prospects already have some sort of relationship with you. They know who you are and what you do. If you haven't kept in touch with them, which is my assumption here, then their might not be a very strong affinity, but at least they're not a complete stranger. As we've discussed many times before, marketing to a list of people that know you is far more cost effective and yields better return on investment than marketing to cold lists.

Granted, you have to do cold marketing in order to build your warm list, but if you have an in-house list of old prospects and past year clients, you should always invest more time and money into marketing to that group than in doing new lead generation. This applies to any service you are offering, not just tax return preparation.

So now that you understand why you need to compile

this list, where are we going to gather the data from? Since you're running a tax practice, you're probably used to keeping records around for a while. We're going to scour those records in order to compile the necessary lists.

If you've been using a computerized appointment scheduling system for any length of time, then you already have a good base to start from. Your tax preparation software may also have a function that allows you to export a client list. Your tax software won't include people that cancelled appointments or simply didn't show up, however, so you'll need to look through appointment books or the scheduling system in order to find those names.

If you only recently switched to using tax software, you have a much more daunting task ahead of you. It is worth going through your old paper files in order to obtain information regarding clients that may not be in any of your electronic records, if those computer files are only a couple years old due to the e-file mandate.

How far back should you go? The honest answer is to go as far back as you have paper files. If you've been in practice for a while, there are probably old tax returns in your archives that you prepared a decade ago, and haven't seen the person since. While it might sound like overkill to go back that far, the fact is that you want as comprehensive of a list as possible.

If nothing else, I would suggest going back at least three years. Somebody that came to you three years ago, and didn't come back for the following tax season, is more likely to still be in your area than somebody from 10 years ago. They are also more likely to remember you, and you're also going to be within the 1040-X window in case you need to amend a return prepared by whomever they went to after you. The amended return strategy is a great way to win back customers (it's been a major customer driver for H&R Block the last few years).

In the past, if you used any sort of lead tracking card or referral cards, consider pulling those out again and match them up against returns actually completed. Those that you did returns for will go on your inactive client list, and those that were referred to you but that did not have a return done will go on your warm prospect list.

As you can see, the general idea is that you want to use any source available to compile your house list. This can be a time consuming endeavor if you are new to electronic filing in particular, but if you were ever going to go through this exercise, right now is the time to do it. The current calm before the first peak storm is the perfect time of year to be doing this, especially if you have added seasonal tax staff that are sitting idle right now.

Remember, the goal is create multiple lists. They can all be in the same CRM database or Excel spreadsheet, but you need to segregate the names using some field flag or indicator in a column as follows:

1. Clients for whom you prepared a return last year.

2. Clients for whom you prepared a return prior to

last year. Go back as far as you reasonably can.

3. Cancelled appointments, no call/no shows, and leads/referrals that did not book appointments.

These three categories are your minimum categories. You can obviously separate them further, and you should keep information on hand in order to do so, but these are the three core categories.

This is your house list, and it is the single most important key to a successful tax season.

In the future, I will refer to these three categories as follows: active clients, inactive clients, and warm prospects. These three categories really form the base of all tax season marketing for established tax preparation practices.

If you're just getting started in private practice and therefore don't have past leads, referrals, and clients to work through, then you need to be in full on new lead generation mode in order to start building your house list.

Client Retention

Client retention is often ignored by tax practitioners. Most people just assume that their existing clients are going to come back. At best, some practitioners send a postcard, letter, or make a phone call to schedule this year's appointment.

If you're not at least doing this, then you are losing a LOT of tax prep business. I would encourage you to examine your roster of clients that came back last year versus the year before, and I'd bet money that there are a lot of missing names in 2013 that visited you in 2012. Why did those people not come back? Because you didn't ask them to.

At the very least, send a letter to your tax season clients every December or January reminding them to schedule an appointment for the coming year. Also, start a client newsletter.

Client Reactivation

When most people lose a client, they don't stop to ask why. This is unfortunate, because most client losses can actually be prevented. In this day and age, even "adequate" customer service is enough to keep somebody coming back, since everybody else is so bad at it. I visited several retail tax franchises in the spring of 2011 in Utah and Colorado, doing my own sort of "mystery shopping", and everywhere I went, the customer service was horrific.

Aside from customer service, another reason that tax firms lose clients year over year is because they don't maintain contact with them throughout the rest of the year. **Your interaction with tax prep clients should not be an annual-only event.**

Maximizing Lifetime Client Value

The best time to start preparing for next time season is right at the end of the last tax season.

Say what?

It's often been said that the best time to get people to pay you more money is immediately after they've already paid you money. This is called an "upsell", and is responsible for as much as 30% of the profits generated by service professionals of all sorts, ranging from auto mechanics to insurance brokers.

When a client is sitting across from you to sign their Form 8453 or pick up their mailable 1040 package is the best possible time to discuss other important service topics, such as tax planning, wealth management, payroll services, business tax preparation, bookkeeping, tax liability resolution, etc.

But on top of that, immediate follow up communication with these clients is invaluable. The "know, like, and trust" factor with your client is at it's highest right when you deliver their tax return to them. It is at this point in time that your client respects you the most…values your knowledge the most…and knows you the best.

What should you send them after meeting with them for the last time during tax season?

If nothing else, they should receive a handwritten thank you note in a nice envelope from you. You can pick these up at the local dollar store 5 or 10 cents each.

But beyond that, this is the perfect time to begin engaging with your clients on a REGULAR BASIS. By regular, I mean at least monthly. **Many professional marketers will suggest a weekly or greater followup program.** This is perfectly valid advice, and is worth following.

To some, myself included, this is a bit excessive and isn't necessary. I personally believe the same results can be achieved with a **"bi-weekly + a bit more" kind of program**.

You'll often see me reference what is called a 33-touch program. Over the course of a year, 33 "touches" (aka, contacts) with your clients and **active prospects that have received a consultation** is highly effective in maintaining and building great relationships with your clients.

You may be wondering, where does this 33 number come from?

In all honestly, this number comes from the real estate world. One of the founders of the Keller Williams real estate brokerage did a significant amount of research in the development of their brokerage marketing program that they created for their agents, and one of the findings was that a 33-touch program over the course of 12 months was the ideal balance between cost effectiveness and long term maintenance of the client relationship and conversion of active prospects to paying clients.

If you have not contacted your clients since you delivered their tax return to them, then **stop what you're doing and send them something RIGHT NOW**. Yes, stop reading this newsletter and go buy little thank you card notes and envelopes at Dollar General or Family Dollar. Seriously, do it, do it now. Send them to your entire client list, your entire dream prospect list, and your entire list of consultations you've conducted in the past 6 months.

By doing this NOW, you are "re-activating" your contact with your lists. Studies show that for each month that goes by in which you don't contact your list, you "lose" 10% of the people on your list to your competitors.

This statistic may not necessarily hold true for long term tax return preparation clients that come back to you each year, but face it: You do lose some people each year no matter what.

Plus, the money you spend to obtain a new active prospect is essentially LOST if you don't do something to follow up with those prospects. Never forget that it costs far more money to obtain a new client or active prospect than it does to keep an existing one.

What is the cost of long-term client/prospect follow up programs?

An effective 33-touch program should cost no more than $50 per client/prospect per year to implement.

What does $25, $33, or even $50 per year per client/prospect get you in return? Let's say that your 33-

touch program results in the referral of 1 new tax preparation client from each of 10 existing tax prep clients (this is a really low referral rate, by the way).

At a national average of over $250 per itemized 1040 return per year, you spent $250 to $500 to obtain $233, right? Wrong. That referral is going to keep coming back to you year after year, and is actually worth several thousand dollars to you over the course of the business relationship.

On top of that, your touch program kept your 10 original clients coming back the next year. If it cost $50 per year to get them to come back and spend $50, that is a worthwhile ROI.

In reality, also keep in mind that you should simply be adding the annual cost of your touch program to your base tax prep fee.

Are you starting see how a touch program not only pays for itself by keeping your clients coming back, but also generates referrals that pay you more money over the years?

Then consider additional service sales. What if, for every 10 clients you market to year round, one of them per year becomes a high-fee paying client for another service, such as full charge bookkeeping, wealth management, or tax resolution?

Then, your $250-$500 investment per year in a 33-touch program to ten clients becomes worth an ADDITIONAL several thousand dollars <u>PER YEAR</u>.

If you're not convinced by now of the value of such a program, then I'm not quite sure what to say. If the cost of such a program sounds too excessive, then your priorities regarding the long-term health of your client pipeline are misplaced, in my opinion.

Never forget that your clients are your mortgage payment and grocery money. Without them, you're a highly trained and certified homeless bum. Therefore, nurture your clients to the greatest extent possible. They will spend more money with you, bring you their friends that will spend money with you, and continue to spend money with you that they have in the past. There's a pattern of money-spending that comes your direction that you should embrace.

Client Newsletters

Throughout the past several decades, the single most powerful tool for building any sort of service business in the lowly client newsletter. Having a quarterly or, better yet, monthly, newsletter that is printed and mailed to your clients, past clients, and best prospects is the single greatest marketing tool you have at your disposal.

In case you missed it in the last paragraph, let me repeat that list:

Clients, past clients, and best prospects.

And yes, it should be <u>printed</u> and <u>mailed</u>.

Printing and mailing a regular client newsletter has far greater impact on your relationship with clients than an email newsletter does. Of course, I am also going to tell you have to a weekly email newsletter and a blog – these are also important elements in maintaining client contact, but not nearly as important as sending them something in the mail.

Getting Our Clients Back

To summarize, the two biggest reasons that tax practitioners lose tax prep clients is because of poor customer service, and lack of regular contact with customers. Assuming that you have fixed these two issues, the next logical question is this: **How do we reactivate old clients?**

Never forget that customers are expensive to acquire. Therefore, the cheapest customer you'll ever get is a repeat customer. In your tax files, you most likely have many, many clients that did not come back to you in 2013 to have their 2012 tax return filed. This applies to both 1040 and 1065/1120 returns, by the way.

What you should do is comb through your old tax files, going back as far as you've been in practice, and compile a list of EVERY client you've EVER had.

From this list, you're going to REMOVE the pain in the neck clients that you either fired or that you should have fired and were glad that they left. In general, if a client is marginal on this item, I would suggest removing them. We're not trying to create headaches, we're trying to grow a business that allows us to be "tax happy".

Then, you're going to go through your 2013 returning clients and remove them from this list, also.

What you're left with is a list, hopefully with addresses, telephone numbers, and perhaps even emails, of past clients that you WANT to return.

You are going to write each of these people a letter, expressing the fact that you miss them, and want them to come back. You're going to mention the fact that your customer service has improved, your tax prep turnaround time is faster, and any other service-level improvements you've made in your firm.

You're then going to bribe them to come back. Make them an offer they can't refuse. Perhaps it's 50% off preparation of their 2013 return. Maybe it will be 3 free months of payroll service. Perhaps a $75 donation to the local charity of their choice. Or maybe a free mid-year tax planning checkup.

Whatever it takes, you are going to offer an <u>ethical bribe</u> to get your old clients to return.

After making that initial offer, you're then going to add those folks to your client newsletter. Again, this newsletter should be sent at least quarterly, if not monthly. It's worth every dime in the long run.

Note: Be sure to remove the names and addresses of people that moved away, based on the return mail you get. If you want to save money and get sophisticated, and it's a large list, you should use a "data hygiene" service to check addresses against the USPS National Change of Address (NCOA) database.

Thirty days after sending the first letter, you're going to remove the names of the people that responded, and send a second letter to the remaining old clients that are on the list. This is going to be their "second notice" letter, and will be much like the first letter, but with more of a "I'm concerned because I haven't heard from you" sort of tone.

Thirty days letter, do it again, but stamp this letter with "Final Notice" across the top, and word it accordingly.

This client reactivation strategy has been successfully used by thousands of small businesses across the country, and has generated billions upon billions of dollars in revenue. It is by no means a new strategy. In fact, it's at least 60 years old. But marketing tactics like this stick around, and get shared from industry to industry, because of the fact that they work.

You should engage in a client reactivation campaign first, before you ever even consider doing new lead generation marketing. It is so much cheaper to get old clients to come back than to find and nurture new leads, that it would be downright foolish to implement any other form of marketing without doing this first.

BIG IDEA #3: DIRECT MAIL IS FAR FROM DEAD

It's amazing how many people "try" direct mail, and then proclaim that it doesn't work.

Unfortunately, most people's idea of "trying" direct mail is to send a few hundred letters using peel-and-stick printed labels with an indicia mark (the pre-paid post mail permit mark used in place of stamps).

When following this approach, you come into the first and biggest barrier of direct mail. When most people sort their mail, they do so by sorting it into "A" pile mail and "B" pile mail.

"A" pile mail is stuff that looks interesting, is of a personal nature, or is important, like bills and paychecks.

"B" pile mail goes straight into the trash can.

When you send direct mail that looks like junk mail, guess which pile it's going into?

Over the past 8 years, I've been heavily involved in the use of direct mail for several different types of projects. It has always fascinated me that different groups of people respond differently to different types of mail, and response even differently so based on how it is sent and what it looks like.

For most of those years, postcards have been my

workhorse. The theory behind postcards is that they are cheap (about half the cost of sending a letter), and you don't have to do anything in order to get them to open your marketing piece – it's already open!

Getting a good response from postcards requires sending more than one. It is not uncommon for me or a business partner to send sequences of 8, 12, even 52 postcards.

For **tax preparation**, it is cost effective to send weekly postcards to a target neighborhood surrounding your tax practice for the entire duration of tax season. From early January through the filing deadline in April, sending 16 offers once per week via postcard to 1,000 homes immediately surrounding your office will cost about $6,200, but only needs to bring in 25 to 40 tax return clients (depending on your fees) in order to recoup that cost.

A 4% response rate might sound like an impossible number to hit, but with a 16-week mailing program with a strong offer to your prospects (such as discounts, refer-a-friend bonuses, etc.) should bring in closer to a double-digit response rate.

You're making an offer for a valuable service that most people are going to use anyway, during the time of year that they are looking for it. It's about as no-lose of a proposition as you can get.

With the advent of the US Postal Service's Every Door Direct Mail program, this method has actually become even more cost effective. EDDM allows you to send the same mailing piece to every home in a carrier route at reduced postage rates. This makes it simple and affordable to saturate your neighborhoods of choice on a regular basis before and during tax season.

To get into the EDDM program, you can work with a printing company that is set up to work with the program, or you can even do it all online through the USPS online mailing system at Click2Mail.com.

Your Friends At ValPak and MoneyMailer

Would you like to get your mail piece into the hands of 10,000 people for only $400 to $800?

ValPak and MoneyMailer are franchised coupon envelope services that are found in most cities across America. They tend not to exist in rural areas and small towns, but cities with populations in the six digits typically will have one of these franchises, or a comparable local company.

The general idea with these companies is that they send a monthly envelope containing coupons and other offers to demographically divided lots of 10,000 homes. You purchase an insert in one or more block of these 10,000 homes.

Depending on your area of the country, a single insert into their oversized envelopes will run about $400 to $800. This means that you can get your message into homes for only four to eight cents each. In direct mail, this is quite a bargain.

It is quite surprising the number of households that get their monthly coupon envelope and sit down and sort through ever insert that is included. During tax season, the presence of your compelling offer on your insert will be timely. The IRS and the mainstream media do a great job of reminding people that it's tax season, so it's naturally on everybody's mind from January-April.

Most coupon mailers in large metropolitan areas sell out several months in advance, so be sure to book yours well ahead of time. I would highly encourage you to test this marketing medium, as it is extremely affordable.

I would suggest signing up to include your insert in every mailer for all of tax season, January through April (inclusive). Commit to testing this in your local market for an entire season one year, and evaluate whether it has a long-term place in your marketing arsenal for future years.

How do you get around mail screening?

Mail screening is an unavoidable issue. It's been an issue since the day the first direct mail marketing piece was ever sent. It's also an issue with telemarketing. Mail will always be screened by the employee or household member whose responsibility it is to get the mail — it's inevitable.

Is it possible to entirely eliminate mail screening? No, not a chance. Can you reduce it? Of course. **The level of direct mail screening goes down as the cost to send it** goes up.

Whenever I've sent marketing materials via FedEx, it's almost guaranteed to get through the screener to the recipient. I said "almost". Yes, even sending things in a FedEx box does not guarantee your intended recipient will ever actually see it. But it's going to be 98% or so. Of course, you're also paying a pretty penny for that open rate.

Sending it USPS Priority Mail will increase open and read rates.

Sending it in specialty envelopes that look "official", but can still be sent first class, will increase read rates.

Using greeting card or stationary size and color envelopes will increase read rates.

Using a handwritten address and a real stamp will increase read rates.

I'm a big fan of sending postcards, since postcards have the highest response rate of any direct mail type (easily 2x to 3x the response rate of letters if done properly). However, postcards also have a significantly higher screening rate.

Why is this? Because postcards don't need to be opened: Your marketing message is right on the postcard for the screener to read, so they can trash it if they don't think the intended recipient wants to see it. **Postcards are the easiest thing to screen, and thus have the highest** screening rate.

Postcards are still my favorite way to do *mass market* direct mail, however. Why? Because it's so cheap to do multi-hit sequential mailings with them. It's a matter of shear numbers: The more folks I can reach out to with my budget, the more prospects I have to work with.

It all depends on your marketing objective. If you're mass marketing your tax services to everybody and anybody, then you can send the cheapest multi-postcard sequences to all of them, very affordably. Postcards are perfect with EDDM in particular.

If, on the other hand, you're only after a very specific type of client, then you need to step things up and use more expensive mailers. Same marketing budget, different objective. You don't send a postcard sequence when you're trying to get specific types of higher fee clients, such as high net worth taxpayers that you also want to offer wealth management services to.

Your direct mail sequences need to be at least 4 weeks in length, preferably 8 or 12, spanning across the entirety of tax season. Frequency and consistency really are the keys to successful direct mail.

Quick 'n' Dirty Direct Mail Primer

If you've never researched direct mail before, here are some key pointers to keep in mind off the top of my head:

1. The purpose here is to GET AN APPOINTMENT, not sell your services in the letter.

2. Follow up with phone calls the day of or the day after your prospect should have received the letter - to SET THE APPOINTMENT.

3. Letters with handwritten addresses are opened about 3x more often than printed labels.

4. A compelling headline in your letter is the single greatest key to response AFTER getting them to open it. It is worth researching the internet for "direct marketing headline banks" to get examples of successful headlines from other people, and modify them to your needs.

5. The goal in direct mail is a 2% response rate - hit that and you're golden!

6. Direct mail works best with "multi-hit" campaigns. E.g., send a first letter, then a couple weeks later send another one to people that didn't respond, saying, "2nd notice - we didn't hear from you" or something like that.

7. Make a limited time offer in your letter. Offer them a report, a book, a seminar, something of value -- but always assign a deadline.

If you're on a limited budget, tip number three above can

be applied quite effectively to give you the marketing octane boost you need. This technique requires a lot of manual labor, but it is highly effective. Instead of mass producing your mail pieces, each one of them is essentially a one-off.

Using Word or a similar program, you mail merge your marketing piece to personalize it, which engages readers. Then, you **mail it in a hand-addressed envelope, with a real stamp, and a goofy return address label** (I like to use SpongeBob Squarepants return address labels – don't judge, it works!).

A hand-addressed envelope with a real stamp and interesting return address label doesn't look like junk mail. Instead, it looks like a personal letter. Even more so if you mail it using a greeting-card sized envelope, rather than a #10 business envelope. This type of letter automatically goes into the "A" mail pile, and is nearly guaranteed to get opened. By getting opened, it crosses the single biggest hurdle to direct mail success.

Why might this technique be more successful than postcards?

Once somebody opens this type of letter, they feel almost compelled to read it, since they bothered to take the time to rip it open and pull it out of the envelope.

Don't forget that direct mail is an ever changing situation, despite being one of the oldest direct response marketing media. Direct mail requires constant testing. Even when you have something that is working really well for you, you still need to be testing new ideas against your current control.

So, to recap, here are the methods for doubling or tripling your direct mail response rates:

- Mail out lengthy sequences of postcards or letters to the same list.
- In highly competitive markets, test the timing of your mailings to get maximum response.
- Start using alternative types of mailers, such as self-addressed envelopes with real stamps or jumbo, full-color postcards.

As mentioned earlier, direct mail is a constantly changing and fickle beast. However, direct mail is still highly effective – has been for a hundred years, and probably will be for 100 more. The cost of customer acquisition is on par with telemarketing when you include commissions paid to salespeople, and can be ramped up or down on your whim.

Even if you do small volumes of direct mail, it's still better than doing none. Just be sure to mail each person on your list more than once. In addition to that, make sure you have a prospect follow up system in place to maintain contact with people that call you, but that don't schedule a tax prep appointment right away.

Getting At New Residents

When people move a significant distance from one city to another, they leave behind a plethora of trusted service providers.

They lose everything from their hair stylist and dentist to their favorite grocery store and taco truck. Within certain "verticals" (niche industries), such as chiropractic and real estate, marketing to these recent movers is a time honored tradition. In other industries, it's almost unheard of.

Well, it's time you heard of it. "New movers" mailing lists are one of the most common mailing lists for many professions to market their services to. Why? Because new people in town are establishing relationships with all new service providers. Because of that, *new movers lists are consistently one of the most profitable mailing lists for many industries to market to.*

A new movers list is a compiled list, based on change of address data and home sales data. Every mailing list broker under the sun offers some version of such lists, and some are better than others. Because of it's popularity, it's also one of the cheaper lists to acquire. Many list brokers, including InfoUSA.com (that's where I get such lists from), will even let you select how far somebody moved, which is important for us. A move of 4 miles probably won't necessitate a change in tax professional, but 50 or 200 miles probably will.

If you are looking for business customers, there are similar lists you can purchase of businesses that have moved, or brand new businesses. New business lists in particular are regularly marketed to for payroll services by the big companies such as ADP, but they are rarely contacted by small, local tax, bookkeeping, accounting, or payroll firms. This entire strategy will work equally well for that market.

If I do a search right now for new movers into the Vancouver, WA area that have moved at least 50 miles, infoUSA tells me that an average of 291 new households per month meet that criteria. That's almost 3,500 people per year -- and I have the opportunity to be the first (and probably the ONLY) tax professional contacting these 3,500 people to have their tax return done in my office.

Even with a mediocre response rate, that can create a compelling addition to seasonal tax prep revenue.

What will it cost me to contact 291 new people each month? About $115, using postcards. It only takes one paid tax return to make up for all of that. Not a bad investment. And the best part is that the response rate should be higher, because I'm not contacting them to sell tax services. **I'm contacting them to invite them to a free event.**

So what do we have so far? We have our reason for contacting people (the event), and we have a list of people to contact that are significantly more likely to respond than the average person (because they are new to the area and have a need). What's next? Do a mailing!

Event Invitation Postcards

Event invitation postcards are simple and easy. All you

need to do is welcome people to the neighborhood, and invite them to your event. These are simple, 4.25 x 6 inch standard postcards, with just a simple invitation on the front, and the mailing address and return address on the front. It really doesn't get any simpler than that.

I use Click2Mail.com for most of my direct mail. This is the US Postal Service contractor for online printing and postage.

If you present your event as a compelling enough offer, you will get people registering. Response rates in the double digit percentages have been achieved using this method. Mailing 300 new movers for $115 and getting anywhere from three to 60 registrants is awesome -- because that means you have that many new prospects. Will they become client? No, probably not. But having these warm prospects that have spent time face to face with you, no matter how small the gathering, is very powerful.

What's all this talk about "events"?

People love events. It's something inherent in the American culture, I think. We love BBQ's, tailgate parties, birthday parties, our seasonal holidays -- pretty much any reason to get together. Corporate cultures love their meetings, and the seminar industry just as big as ever, despite the economic downturn. Webinars are just as popular, and growing every day.

An event brings people together for a common reason. At

an event, even if it's full of complete strangers, there is usually something that ties everybody together. That reason might be an interest in growing their businesses, securing their financial futures, a passion for the a sports team, or their kids all play soccer together. Think about the last time you attended a seminar or industry conference, why you went, and what you got out of it. Those are the reasons people attend events.

Events are more than just an excuse to get together, however. Events are an opportunity for us to learn, grow, and achieve.

Holding regular events is a powerful way to solidify your relationship with prospects. Your events can help people in numerous ways, not just via the tax and accounting services you offer.

What kind of events am I talking about? The occasional client appreciation party is a good one, yes, but more specifically I'm referring to educational events. Monthly seminars on various financial topics, from real estate and mortgages to asset protection and wealth management. There are scores of topics you can cover in monthly seminars.

The best part is that you can invite trusted colleagues in other professions to come in and present information of value to your prospects and clients. Make sure the information is 90% educational, and give your guest presenter a few months to talk about themselves and their services, and you can get a free speaker.

By scheduling and holding regular events, you have something powerful: *Something to always be inviting people to.*

Whenever you meet people, and in all of your marketing, you will always have an opportunity to invite people to meet with you face to face. Since people do business with people they know, like, and trust, these face to face encounters are invaluable for getting people to know you better, and appreciate what you are offering them.

Schedule a regular event. You can hold this in your own office, a local restaurant, or in a community room (check your local library and government offices -- many have public meeting space available for free or very low cost). If you want something more formal, negotiate a good rate with a local hotel for a small meeting room, and be sure to ask for a discount because you'll be back every month.

Then, use these events as a cornerstone of your marketing. Everybody you meet gets an invite. Chamber of Commerce networking luncheon? Everybody gets an invite. Web inquiry for your services? Yes, they get an email newsletter, but they also get an invite.

Just so you know, this particular strategy was perfected within the network marketing industry. Every weekly "opportunity meeting" for an MLM company uses this principle in order to introduce new people to the income opportunity. This method has sold billions of dollars MLM products and packages over the decades, and is still used successfully today.

Long Term Prospect Follow Up

Long term prospect follow up is a subject that I cover extensively elsewhere. Suffice it to say, however, that you should be following up with these prospects on at least a monthly basis, until they either tell you to stop or you get returned mail, bounced emails, and disconnected phone.

These prospects should receive invitations to your other future events. They should come to your client appreciation parties. They should receive your monthly client newsletter. They should get your email updates, birthday cards, anniversary cards, Thanksgiving cards, coupons, special offers, and everything else that should be part of your regular client and prospect touch program.

If you've been looking for one of the most effective ways to get new prospects, and new tax preparation clients in particular, then this is one of the most powerful methods you can use to achieve this. It's a dirt cheap lead generation strategy, but pays massive dividends in the long run for your local tax practice.

BIG IDEA #4: LEVERAGE PROFESSIONAL RELATIONSHIPS

It's no secret that the single best source of clients is **referrals**. However, most practitioners think about referrals only in terms of getting them from your existing clients (which we'll cover in the next chapter). You should do that, of course, but there is another referral source that you may not have given much thought to:

Your professional network.

Now, I'm not just talking about your tax, accounting, or legal colleagues. I'm talking about other professional colleagues that associate with your ideal clients. For example, if your ideal client happens to be high income taxpayers, then you should start associating with financial planners, asset managers, stockbrokers, and insurance folks.

Your professional network is one of the most valuable assets in your tax business. Unfortunately, most tax professionals ignore this incredible referral source entirely, which means that they are leaving tremendous amounts of money on the table. Let's look at how to plug this particular revenue leak.

Your Existing Network

Let's start with your existing network. This generally consists of the people that you went to college with, have met at professional conferences and events, etc. As the old saying goes, "Birds of a feather flock together." In other words, professionals tend to congregate.

When was the last time you made a conscious effort to connect with your fellow tax professionals? What about your college connections?

These sorts of relationships do, unfortunately, deteriorate over time. Thankfully, however, we have two amazing tools these days that provide an excuse to rekindle those long-lost connections: **LinkedIn** and **FaceBook**.

I'm personally not a big fan of social media. Heck, I don't even have a LinkedIn account. My take is that "social media" is just the current trendy buzzword for the same thing that's existed since 1993, the thing I more commonly refer to as "the web".

So, I do not view social media as a panacea of awesomeness and lead generation heaven. Social media sites are nothing but web sites, and all they do is the same thing all other web sites do: Post and link content across the web.

With all that said, however, LinkedIn and Facebook provide an interesting ability that, offline, would be creepy and weird. With LinkedIn and Facebook, we have a tool that grants us societal permission to reestablish contact with long lost friends. If you have a LinkedIn profile but don't really use it, then this is a highly valuable use of that technology.

Connect with your old accounting or law classmates. Connect with people you've met at conferences, seminars, CPE/CLE classes, etc.

Reestablish these contacts online now, so that you can legitimately reestablish these relationships offline later.

Establishing stronger connections with your past and current professional networking contacts is the beginning to growing a referral-based practice.

Growing Your Professional Network

Once you've reestablished contact with your old professional contacts, it's time to start looking at how to grow your professional network.

Growing your professional network is really about nothing more than being a social butterfly. Your colleagues are all around, and as mentioned earlier, professionals like to stick together due to the common thread between them. Basically, you need to start sticking your neck out and being more social at the events where you have an opportunity to meet up with professional colleagues.

Think about all the places you can meet other tax professionals:

- Live continuing education classes.
- Association annual conventions.
- State or local association meetings.
- Marketing seminars.
- Professional working group meetings.

Notice here that the emphasis is on LIVE events.

Basically, all you're doing is *actively participating in your profession*, which is something you're probably already doing. The key difference, however, is that you should be using these opportunities as a chance to get to know people, and make meaningful connections on a friendly, social level.

When you meet new colleagues, be sure to exchange business cards. Add this new person to your professional contact directory, and also add them online as a connection on LinkedIn. I'm also going to suggest investing in the relationship on a live basis, which we'll discuss in the next section.

Strengthening Relationships

Once you've established your professional network, you need to work on strengthening those professional relationships. Never forget that people do business with, and *refer business to*, people that they **know, like and trust**.

Nothing is more important than building this know-like-trust factor. Everything we do in marketing to find clients is all about establishing this.

Getting to know people better is largely a direct result of spending time with them. One of the best things you can do to strengthen relationships is to engage with people, and not just online. I'm talking in person and over the phone.

You should strive to meet regularly with those associates

in your professional network. Meeting for breakfast, lunch, or coffee is always a good bet. Pick up the phone every day and call a few folks on your networking list. This group of people really should be folks you want to hang out with, and that you count as friends.

And what do you do with friends? You have barbecues, grab lunch, play golf, get the families together. These are the similar, even identical things you should be doing with your professional colleagues. Don't forget the Christmas cards, birthday cards, and anniversary cards, too.

In other words, view your relationship with your professional colleagues just as you would with your ideal prospects, high paying clients, and even your friends. It's a "long tail" method of marketing, but the results can be incredibly powerful (and lucrative).

Expanding Your Sphere With Other Groups

Finding a way to meet more people that you can associate with is sometimes considered difficult, but it's really not. What you want to find are not necessarily more tax professionals, but other people that are **well connected**.

For purposes of building a referral-based business, you are seeking quality introductions to other people that can refer you business.

Now, you're not just building relationships for the

purpose of generating business. That would be disingenuous and would be detrimental to building relationships based on trust.

These type of folks will usually be like-minded with you in some regard. More specifically, I suggest that you seek out other entrepreneurially minded folks. Investors, business owners, and professionals from other industries are all excellent referral sources.

These type of people are typically well connected in the community, with their own large spheres of influence. They know other business owners, and numerous individuals, any number of whom may be in need of tax preparation, tax planning, or tax representation.

How do you connect with these types of folks, and get to know them? Just a few examples:

- Chamber of Commerce events
- Local leads groups (such as BNI)
- Regional trade shows
- Civic organizations (Rotary Club, Elks, etc)
- Meetup.com small business groups

All of these places exist largely for the purpose of meeting people, and discussing items of common interest. Participate in such groups, be active within the communities that are of interest to you, and build your network outside of our profession in this way.

Mastermind Groups

Start getting together with your expanding sphere of connections in small group sessions to discuss business. You'll be meeting a lot of business people, and various business owners and professionals will have interest in various topics. Form weekly or monthly groups with those individuals that are interested in particular topics.

Getting together to discussion a particular topic is POWERFUL for building the know/like/trust factor that I mentioned earlier. You can get together once a month with one group to discuss sales, another group to discuss Internet marketing, another group to discuss investing, etc.

The time you spend building these relationships, over the long haul, could *literally* be the only marketing you ever need to do to grow your practice.

Generating Referrals

So, you're creating these powerful relationships with your colleagues, and you're building other relationships with business owners and other associates through multiple methods. So how do you actually generate referrals from these relationships?
This is the easiest part of the process: **Everybody that knows you should know what you do and what you're looking for in terms of ideal clients.**

As a natural consequence of building strong relationships, and making sure that everybody knows your area of specialization and a basic idea of your idea client, referral will come.

You do need to be specific about what kind of clients you are looking for, and make sure your friends know. If you are looking for small business owners having problems paying their taxes every month, then make sure that this is known.

Cultivating a network of powerful referral connections is one of best things you could ever do to grow a local tax practice.

Referrals tend to make the best clients, pay on time more often, and become lifetime clients. While I consider direct mail and Internet marketing to be the best ways to rapidly grown an "instant" client base, or for growing a nationwide client base, simply nothing beats the power of a personal referral network for steadily (and inexpensively) growing a local tax practice.

BIG IDEA #5: ASK FOR REFERRALS

The absolute best source of new clients is to obtain referrals from your existing clients. People tend to refer other people that are much like themselves, so asking your best clients for referrals will generally result in new clients much like themselves.

Asking your existing clients for referrals can be done in a simple and stress-free manner, and can even involve an ethical bribe.

If you don't already have a **Refer-A-Friend** program in place, I would highly encourage you to start one. Here is how these programs work:

1. Existing clients receive a letter in the mail or a card at their tax prep appointment, asking for the names of five people they know that might be interested in your services.

2. The client giving the referral receives a set amount of money, typically $20 to $50, for each paying client that comes in from their referrals.

3. As an incentive for coming in, their friend receives some discount, often the same amount, for coming in. For example, both the client and the friend receive $25.

4. An additional incentive is provided to your client if all five of their referrals become paying clients. For example, they may receive $25 per person, but

an additional $25 if all five come in, for a total of $150.

I like to see these programs operated in such a manner that the client giving you the referrals actually ends up getting their services essentially free for giving you X number of referrals.

The dollar amounts provided here are examples only. If your average 1040 fee is higher, then adjust these numbers upwards to make it more compelling for your clients to refer people they know.

Presenting this at your tax prep appointments is extremely simple and low-pressure. While you are entering data or reviewing documents, simply say, "Are you familiar with our Refer-A-Friend program?" Then either hand them the brochure and/or briefly explain it to them.

If you can get your client to fill out the referral card right there on the spot, you are more likely to actually get referrals.

BIG IDEA#6: CHOOSE THY CLIENTS WISELY

This is a hard pill for just about all tax professionals to swallow: *Some clients simply aren't worth your time.*

Not all clients are created equally. The simple fact of the matter is that you're in business to make a living, and some clients simply are not profitable.

At the same time, some clients are such a pain in the neck that you don't want to deal with them. Some clients suck up an inordinate amount of our time, and they need to go elsewhere.

What exactly constitutes an ideal tax return client for your practice?

I believe that ideal clients share three common traits:

1. They are a pleasure to work with. At a minimum, we don't dread taking their phone calls or seeing them walk into the office.

2. They pay their fees in full and on time, and recognize that occasional fee increases are simply part of business.

3. They are clients for multiple services that you offer.

You'll notice that two of these traits relate directly to two other Big Ideas discussed in this book. This is not a coincidence.

Within your marketing plan, you should assemble a list of ideal prospects, and create a special marketing effort specifically aimed at them that is on top of your regular marketing efforts for your more "run of the mill" clients.

This deal client prospecting campaign is established with the distinct goal of creating a relentless, never ending effort to literally have 100% of these prospects become your client. For most firms, this list won't be that long. It may run from as little as a dozen ideal prospects, to at most a couple hundred.

Who is on your ideal prospect list? It really depends on the nature of your practice and your areas of specialization. Here are some examples of ideal prospect lists:

- All companies within a 25-mile radius of your office with 50 to 250 employees.

- All tax debtors within a 4-state region that owe more than $500,000 to the IRS and earn 7 figures annually.

- Owners of homes assessed at greater than $1.2 million within one ZIP code that are also boat owners.

- 941 tax debtors owing more than $150,000 and annual revenue greater than $5 million within your greater metropolitan area.

- Families in your city with more than $2 million in liquid assets.

As you can see, these prospects are special because they have specific characteristics that are desirable to us as clients. They represent high-value clients that will pay us substantial fees and will stay with us as clients for years and years.

These high-value prospects are worth a special marketing effort that essentially never ends. I would suggest a marketing effort that contacts these ideal prospects at least monthly, if not bi-weekly or even weekly, with some sort of "touch". Since the cost of a typical touch is only $1, or even less, you can market to a list of 100 such prospects on a weekly basis for only $5,200 per year, which is a drop in the bucket compared to the value of of one such client in terms of the fees that just ONE of them will pay you over the course of a business relationship.

What does a year-long, weekly touch program look like? It can be as simple as this:

- 12 monthly newsletters (covering tax advice, asset

protection, wealth management, etc.)

- Bi-weekly postcards offering a free report, briefing, webinar, live seminar, interview recording, etc.

- One phone call per month

- Birthday card, anniversary card, Thanksgiving card

- Invitation to a private client event (BBQ, family fun day, etc.)

As you can see, this marketing program is neither elaborate nor expensive, but is worth every dime. When you obtain a client that pays you several thousand dollars per year in fees for several years, this entire marketing program is paid for forever.

If you don't have an active campaign to target your ideal prospects, above and beyond your regular lead generation marketing, then I would highly encourage you to identify your special prospects and begin marketing to them.

BIG IDEA #7: RAISE YOUR FEES

The subject of fees is one of the most contentious things to bring up when in a group of tax professionals. All of us have different opinions on the subject of fees, and we tend to defend those opinions ruthlessly.

I tend to assert that practitioners don't charge enough. Not only are fees not high enough to begin with, practitioners do a lot of work for free. The little things that you do as favors for clients here and there add up.

Think about it, how many "one quick question…" phone calls do you get from clients that turn into 10 minute…30 minute…hour long conversations – not to mention the disruption on your work flow and productivity for the day (bonus Big Idea: Don't answer your phone during other scheduled activities, such as other client work, marketing time, etc.).

"I can't raise my rates," I hear you say. "I'll lose all my clients, nobody will pay higher rates in this economy," you exclaim.

In reality, you couldn't be more wrong.

First, when was the last time you DID raise your rates? If you never have, or it's been more than a couple years, then you're long overdue anyway.

Second, people will, and consistently DO, pay higher fees for the services they use. People understand that the cost of doing business goes up. Your cost of living goes up, your payroll increases. Inflation is part of economic growth (and the economy is growing, just slower these days).

Third, if you take a serious look at your client base, you will most likely find that two instances of the Pareto Principle are in effect at your firm. The Pareto Principle, also known as the 80/20 rule, states that roughly 80% of your results come from 20% of your efforts. What this means in your practice is that roughly 80% of your profits probably come from just 20% of your clients. Similarly, 80% of your headaches probably come from 20% or less of your clients.

It's time to critically analyze where your revenues are coming from, on a client by client basis. It's also time to look at your headache clients, the ones that piss you off the most, take advantage of you the most, etc. One of the effects of raising your rates is that these clients tend to be the ones that go away, not the ones that are your best clients.

The relationship you have with your best clients will weather a rate increase. In fact, it's not uncommon for your best clients to tell you they're surprised you haven't raised rates sooner, given the level of service you provide them. Your bad clients, on the other hand, will take their headache elsewhere, which should be just fine by you, as these clients tend to consume more of your resources than they produce.

Analyze your clients down to the dollars they generate and the resources in your practice that they consume. Overtly fire your unprofitable clients by sending them letters informing them that, since you are losing money on them, you need to charge them more. Make it a significant price increase, such as 50% or even double. If they pay it, then good for you. If they don't, then good for you.

For the rest of your clients, implement a price increase on all your services. As mentioned above, they'll understand. And if not, then they would have left anyway when you eventually had to raise prices anyway.

For new clients, set your pricing at a slight premium for your marketplace. Don't take on new clients that are going to become headache clients because you are the cheapest guy in town. Become the top of the food chain by charging premium prices, and offering premium service.

How To Set Fees

During the process of writing this chapter, the National Society of Accountants released their most recent member fee survey.

This year, among the 1300+ practitioners surveyed, the average fee for an itemized 1040 and state return was

$261. Tack on an extra $142 to $218 for a Schedule D or C, respectively. Average 1120S fees were reported as $761.

I'm definitely glad to see that average tax prep fees among survey respondents are going up. These fees increased ahead of the CPI inflation rate over last year's NSA survey.

Here's what alarms me about the publication of this data, however: At least in various online forums, it prompts fee discussions among practitioners seeking to base their next season fees on these averages.

Right now, in the comment sections of several blogs and on a couple of tax/accounting discussion boards, this survey is causing practitioners to engage in unhealthy discussions about what their fees "ought to be".

I want to do my part to try and nip this in the bud right now. Let me state right here and now, unequivocally and without apology: **Your fees should NEVER be based on what other people charge.**

It's one of the biggest mistakes that ALL business owners make, but it's especially visible within professional service fields such as our own. In almost every field of endeavor, new business owners look to what their competitors are doing, and base their pricing, marketing, and operations on what everybody else is doing.

You already know that I advocate doing marketing in ways that your competitors don't. But I feel the same way about pricing.

Your fees should be based on the value that you bring to the marketplace. If your fees are too high, the marketplace will let you know. But it's better to start high and come down, than to start low and have to fight the uphill battle when you raise fees.

By far the most obvious arena where I see this is in tax prep fees versus hourly rates. Most practitioners have an hourly rate floating around inside their brain, even if they don't bill by the hour, and this is perfectly fine. The problem comes when their tax preparation fees are significantly less than their hourly rate, regardless of whether that hourly rate is stated or not.

Here's an example. Let's say your hourly rate is $250. Let's also say that your base rate for an itemized 1040 is also $250, and that you charge an extra $150 for a Schedule C. That's $400 for this example return. But after all the work that goes into the actual return, particularly on creating a P&L for the C from bank statements and random receipt from your client, you're actually four hours into this entire return.

At your hourly rate, this should be a $1,000 return. But your fee is only $400. While some practitioners reading this will have charged the client the $1,000, an alarming number of tax professionals will only charge the $400!

This is the danger of using survey data and competitive shopping (calling around to other firms asking for price quotes, pretending to be a potential client) for setting your own fees. You think that you're taking steps to be competitive in the marketplace, but you're actually just shooting yourself in the foot.

Survey data has it's place, for sure. As a data junkie, I actually enjoy seeing these numbers. But I caution you against making one of your most important business decisions based on that data.

Your fee structure should be based on how much revenue you want to generate, the value you bring to the marketplace, and your target market's ability to pay the fee. In reality, those are the only three factors that should matter when it comes to setting fees.

Making Up For NOT Raising Fees

Have you not raised fees in several years, and need to bring your fees up to where they should be?

If you have several year's worth of fee increases that you've missed, you've got two different routes you can go. After analyzing your revenue and expenses, and deciding where you want your fees to be, you can either do it all at once, or phase it in over the next few years.

A substantial fee increase at one time has the benefit of

helping you to fire clients that you no longer want. Instead of being afraid to jack up your fees, look at it as the opportunity to get rid of clients that, for some reason or another, you simply don't want to service anymore, but haven't had the heart to tell them. Just explain that you're increasing fees, and refer them to a colleague if they choose not to stay with you.

Personally, I suggest implementing fee increases all at once. But if you need to phase them in, then don't forget to add the current fee increase, plus the fee increase you'll need to add next year for inflation or desired growth. If you're phasing in a 30% increase over three years, but also want to raise 5% per year each year ongoing, then you actually need to increase fees 15% for three years to catch up, then 5% per year thereafter.

BIG IDEA #8: INCREASE EFFICIENCY VIA SYSTEMS

Creating systems is the key to efficiency in anything. If you look at the most efficient companies, the most efficient processes in the world, they all use systems. In my opinion, anything worth doing is worth systemizing.

What items should have a checklist? Consider:

- Somebody is responsible for doing it
- Anything that is done regularly
- It involves marketing or sales
- Client work, client interaction, client retention,
- Referral generation
- Anything that is a revenue driver
- Human resource issues

All of these matters require a checklist.

Checklists are the thing that make my universe go around. Without checklists and systems, my lifestyle simply wouldn't be possible.

For a lot of the tax firms that I work with, they discover that once they implement a systems-based approach to conducting their internal operations, they discover that the work volume that they can handle at the same amount of staff easily doubles, if not triples.

When you can handle a larger client load, guess what happens? Your revenue goes up without any increase in your overhead particularly for staff.

Another great thing about systems is that when everything is done the same way every time, regardless of who is doing it (you, a staff member, a stand-in person doing it while the normal person that does it is on vacation, etc), it provides predictability. Predictability is good, especially for us in the accounting and tax world.

Predictability is the way we want things to work. Predictability leads to a reliable client experience, which is going to help us get referrals. Happy clients are the type that stay with us forever, pay us on time, and refer their friends and family freely.

What about the process of creating checklists? All checklists should have a single, clear, well-defined objective. All checklists should include potential hangups and common errors in completing them.

Nothing is ever too dumb to put on a checklist. For example, my Form 8821 checklist has an entry saying to check the box on line 5 of the form 8821 so that we get copies of notices through the tax information authorization, not just through the power of attorney.

That might seem dumb, but it is a little thing that makes a

big difference later on. Nothing is too dumb to put on a checklist.

Every step of a checklist should have a specific action. Also, communication channels should be integrated into your systems. Different pieces of different checklists need to be able to talk to each other, and I mean that both figuratively and literally.

When you are developing checklists, make sure to include other people. Other people might have good ideas that are worth incorporating into your systems. You should be striving for continuous and never ending improvement (CANI) in your business and particularly in your systems and checklists.

When writing checklists, be sure to use natural breaks in the workflow of a process. Most things that are done sequentially have natural breaks in the work flow. For example, on an IRS form, it is natural to have things go from section to section that are related. So, those create natural breaks in the workflow of filling out that form.

Checklists should always be compiled using simple sentences and words. Anybody with an 8th grade education should be able to understand your checklist. Put things in a logical order and make them easy to follow. Steps in the checklist should not be too wordy, they should not include extraneous details, they should be very simple to follow and logical.

Most checklists should be short, generally a page or less, and they should end with achieving the stated objective for that checklist. If it does not fit on one page or it does not end with achieving a particular objective, then chances are you have a checklist that should actually be broken up into more than one checklist.

Always be sure to reference upstream and downstream checklists. Usually checklists are nested. They branch out and are related to each other.

Here are some additional questions to consider when writing checklists:

1. What milestones do I need to reach to day in order to reach my goals?

2. What metrics do I need to achieve to be working towards my overall goals?

3. What actions have I taken that are preventing me from taking goals that I have set?

4. If I am not feeling motivated, what physical aspects do I need to take in order to become motivated or create momentum?

To summarize the primary points increasing efficiency within your practice:

Eliminate things that you are doing that are not worth doing and that are simply wasting your productive time. Chances are, you are spending too much time checking email. You are spending too much time allowing interruptions into your day. You are spending to much time on Facebook and Twitter. So eliminate those things that just suck up your productive time.

Delegate out tasks that can be done better by an expert or that are below your pay grade. You cannot, I repeat, you cannot make a quarter million dollars a year if you are sitting around doing $10 an hour administrative tasks. It is not going to happen.

Automate routine tasks to the maximum extent possible while maintaining quality. You do not want quality of work and the quality of your client relationships to suffer from automation. But you should take advantage of automation of anything that you possibly can. Many times, automation can actually improve your client's experience. Automation helps you service more clients in less time, which helps increase revenue. With automation, there are fewer errors on forms, more regular client/prospect contact because of CRM systems, fewer missed deadlines.

Systemize everything that you do in your practice regardless of who does it by creating checklists for everything. When you have checklists for running every aspect of your practice, it makes things more efficient, it makes things operate smoother, it allows for a more productive work environment, and I think a more fun environment because everybody knows what everybody needs to do. There is no question about whether Sally needs to be doing this or that what John needs to be doing right now – everybody knows what to do and when because the checklist tells them to.

PROFITABILITY IS A CHOICE

It is my hope that the 8 Big Ideas presented in the preceding chapters have allowed you to see one other, overarching Big Idea, which is that **profitability is a choice**.

You are in business for the purpose of generating a profit. I have yet to meet a single tax practitioner that is in business for any other reason. We may occasionally do pro bono work for some clients, and we may occasionally volunteer our services at places like low income tax clinics. But the reality of being in business for ourselves boils down to being able to keep a roof over our heads and feed our families.

The way that you operate your business, and the **choices** you make in regards to your marketing practices, your fees, the type of clients you choose to work with, etc., all play a massive role in determining whether or not your practice is profitable, and to what degree.

I encourage you to not just put this book on your bookshelf and go about your business as usual, especially during the next tax season. This book is fairly short, and the ideas in it are neither complex nor excessively technical. Most of the ideas contained herein can be implemented with a simple change of procedure within your practice. Other items that require setup, such as creating mailing pieces, take but a few hours at most.

This year, choose profitability for yourself. Have a great tax season!

ABOUT THE AUTHOR

Jassen Bowman is an IRS-licensed Enrolled Agent that specializes in collections representation. Jassen operates the TaxMarketingHQ.com blog, publishes *The Profitable Accountant* practice growth newsletter, and has produced a number of tax resolution and tax marketing training programs. Jassen is also a nationally acclaimed speaker, presenting on marketing and IRS Collections representation CPE topics.

To contact Jassen regarding speaking at conferences and seminars, or to learn more about marketing courses and programs available, please visit:

http://TaxMarketingHQ.com

FREE BONUS

This book is really just the beginning of your journey. In order to support you in your efforts at growing your tax practice, we created a **membership website** that has additional training and resources to help you build your tax resolution practice.

The great news is that access to this site is 100% free. To get access, go to:

www.TaxMarketingHQ.com/bonus

Here is what you'll receive:

- A comprehensive 6-hour video series that introduces you to the essentials of starting and growing a tax resolution practice, including the fundamentals of marketing, client intake, practice management, sales, and tax resolution case work.
- Detailed training on how to find your first tax resolution client.
- How to quote tax resolution fees.
- The world famous *One-Hour Per Day Marketing Plan*.
- Access to complimentary CE/CPE webinars on IRS Collections topics.
- Additional links, resources, and bonuses from the book.
- A few surprises along the way.

You can access everything at:

https://TaxMarketingHQ.com/bonus

Please note that this offer is subject to change or substitution at any time.

www.ingramcontent.com/pod-product-compliance
Lightning Source LLC
Chambersburg PA
CBHW071755170526
45167CB00003B/1043